Manufactured in the United States of America
ISBN 0-8062-5381-9

Contents

MUSING MOMENTS

Memories

The lilting laughter of a brook,
The opening of a flower,
The green trees whisp'ring in the breeze,
A secret, leafy bower.
The joys of happy childhood days,
Long-gone but not forgot
Come back on lonely city nights
When city streets are hot.

A tramp through winter fields of white,
With snow knee-deep and chilling—
Then home to warmth beside the fire,
With love the whole house filling.
The joys of happy childhood days
My heart will ever hold
To comfort me on lonely nights
When city streets are cold.

Joy!

The bluest skies that you can find
Are not on cloudless days.
A tiny little break in clouds
Lets through a bright blue blaze.

It is the same with happiness.
In good times, we're quite content.
But little joys in troubled times
Seem truly heaven-sent.

Suffer the Little Children

A child came laughing to my door,
I welcomed him inside.
He told me funny little jokes.
His smile was quick and wide.

He loved the people in his world,
All nature was his friend.
He slept in peace and woke with joy,
Was glad in sun or wind.

Another day, another boy
Came knocking at my door.
His mouth was drawn and sadly set
By something gone before.

He did not want to talk at all,
But leaned against my chair,
And turned his face away and wept,
Bowed down by childish care.

I gave them all I had to give;
My hand, with tender love,
A sharing of both joy and woe—
And prayers to God above.

Beauty

In the grandeur of the sunset,
In the splendor of the dawn,
In the richness of the plowed field,
In the velvet, grassy lawn,

I can see all kinds of beauty
Fashioned by the hand of God,
From the colors of the rainbow
To the weeds from good black sod.

So it is with God's own children,
Whether grand or simple folk,
All the faces shine with beauty
After they accept His yoke.

Lead My Hand

Once there was a little girl
Who was so very shy—
If anyone should speak to her,
She would not lift her eye.

She loved her Daddy more than most
And blossomed when with him
Like a fragile little flower
On a Spring-time slender stem.

When she reached up to him,
She knew he'd understand
What need she was expressing
With, "Daddy, lead my hand."

Years have passed, and Daddy's gone,
But still she feels secure—
There is no cause for her to fear,
Of this she is quite sure.

She knows her heavenly Father's hand
Will always be right there,
Just as her earthly father's was
To show His love and care.

A Mystery

I do not understand the mystery of:
How and why He created the universe,
But I know He did:

I do not understand the mystery of:
How and why He came as mortal man,
But I know He did:

I do not understand the mystery of:
Why He sacrificed Himself in love,
But I know He did:

I do not understand the mystery of:
His birth, His life, His death, and
His resurrection,
But I know it is true:

I do not understand the mystery of:
How or when He will return,
But I know He will:

I do not understand the mystery of:
His having a home for me in heaven
Where I shall live forever,
But I know He does:

This I do know,
This I do understand,

This I do believe,
And I rejoice:

His Holy Spirit fills my soul with joy and peace.
This comes from my knowledge that the mystery
Is too great for my human mind:

But, someday, "I shall know fully just as
I have been fully known."

I praise the Father, Son, and Holy Spirit:

Amen

Communion

I take the bread and hold it in my hand.
I bow my head and wait.
I take the little cup of wine and feel that it is cold.
My hand is warm and pulsing with the life
given to me by my resurrected Lord.
The wine that represents His blood is
cold—cold—cold: His human blood once ran
warm with love, compassion and pity for all
men—men made in the image of His Father.
who sent Him.
His blood ran warm until man pierced His
brow with thorns, His back with lashes, His
hands and feet with nails, and finally, His pre
cious side with spears of hate.
His human blood ran down His tortured body
to the earth at the foot of the cross. It became
as cold as the hearts of those He came to save.
As I held the cup in my hand, my warmth
could not overcome the cold.
Then I ate the Bread of His body, and drank
the Wine of His blood. I prayed that my heart
would be blessed by His Holy Spirit with the
resurrected warmth of our risen Lord who took
away the cold of death and gave us the
warmth of eternal life.

Amen

The Way Is Narrow

The world predicts my certain doom
As I cross life's raging streams,
Walking narrow logs of faith
To reach my long-held dreams.

I do not seek the crowd's applause
Nor wish for such acclaim.
I want to serve my Lord and King,
Not strive for wealth or fame.

If I can know His will for me
I count the dangers small
Of any ridicule or sneers
Which on my head may fall.

My faith will light the paths I take
In all my future days,
And I shall surely reach at last
His peace, and joy, and praise.

Easter Hope

The tears of our sorrow make heavy the heart,
And bodies are bowed down with grief.
The light of the sun grows dreary and dark,
And weeping will bring no relief.

Our Lord suffered so as He hung on the Cross—
The universe wept for His pain.
But efforts of evil to bring Him to shame
Like the seal on the tomb were in vain.

As the joy that emerged on that Easter morn'
Astonished the mourners who came,
And opened their eyes on that beautiful day
To know, and to call Him by name.

When dark days of sadness come into our lives,
His hands which were torn by the nails
Are ready to lead us out into the light
With love that we know never fails.

Easter Sonnet

Came Easter Morn! The stone was rolled away
When Mary came with spices to anoint
Her Lord ... It was before the break of day,
But grief made heavy heart and weary joint—
Her body ached for every lash He Took—
Her blood seemed turned to water as He bled.
Though blind with tears, she forced herself to look
As He, in agony, bowed low His head.
She could not stop her ears from His last cry.
This woman who, perhaps, had sinned the most
And knew His mercy, wished that she might die,
And her heart broke when He gave up the ghost.
But oh the joy of that bright Easter morn
When Christ—and she—and we—had been reborn!

The Child Is Born

Mother! Mother! Have you heard? There is within the cave back there
A tiny baby boy!

Mother! Mother! Say I may go and ask if I may look on him?
I know 'twould bring me joy.

'Tis said they came and could not find a room in which to stay the night.
I'm glad the cave was bare!

You know I love to hold a babe, and see his little hands and feet,
And touch his baby hair.

But yet—I feel a strange unrest. It seems my heart is being drawn
To go and look on him.

I know not how to describe the way the air seems warm and bright,
And yet the sun looks dim—

It seems some glow is all about—I cannot see, but it is there—
A kind of holy light.

I know not how he calls to me. But this I know. A wondrous child
Came down to earth last night!

The Man Possessed (Mark 5:1-15)

He broke all chains that man could not make,
But Satan's chains he could not break.

"Legions" made of him a slave—
He could not speak, except to rave.

But demons knew when Jesus came
And answered when He asked their name.

They begged Him to withhold His power
And spare them in that awful hour.

At their request—and as a sign—
He let them go into the swine.

The crazed swine were made to flee,
And all met death within the sea.

The man who once had been so wild
Became as gentle as a child.

In stainless clothes he was arrayed,
And those who saw were sore afraid.

They missed the glory of that day
And begged the Christ to go away!

The Promise

There will be days of sadness
As our lives on earth unfold,
But as surely as the warming sun
Dispels the winter's cold

From the sorrows of our lifetime
God's good will comes to pass,
As, quietly in the springtime,
Comes the greening of the grass.

When we say good-bye to loved ones
The skies seem cold and gray,
But they've gone to claim His promise
That all tears He'll wipe away.

Wait with Joy

We sometimes find it very hard
To "Wait upon the Lord"
We find the waiting tiresome,
And let ourselves be bored.

If other people—other things-
Would fit into our schemes
Everything would work quite well,
Or that's the way it seems.

But circumstances are not right,
Time seems to just stand still,
Our plans are foiled on every side—
Till we accept His will.

When we admit His mighty strength,
And our own weakness see,
We then can hope for lasting joy
Because He sets us free.
We find His strength for every task,
He guides us every day.
Then waiting is our greatest joy,
His will our chosen way.

Welcome Spring

The falling rain washed clean my world.
        The leaves were fresh and green.
My eyes beheld more loveliness
        Than they had ever seen.

Each year when winter fades away,
        And buds burst forth in bloom,
I see more beauty than before
        As joy replaces gloom.

I stop and gaze in rapt delight
        At each new sign of Spring.
I breathe a prayer of praise to God
        For every lovely thing.

Growing Old

I'm growing old and find my thoughts
Turn backward through the years.
I still can laugh at many things—
Still feel the sting of tears.

The memories come sharp and clear
Like objects in my hand—
And I am glad for every one,
The lawdry and the grand.

My body is not beautiful,
But what would I disclaim?
I need each part to be a whole,
As pictures need a frame.

Though hands are growing gnarly now,
And knees are not so spry,
My shoulders are not quite so straight,
Nor quite so sharp my eye,

They all combine to make what's me—
Developed through the years.
My soul leaps up and shouts for joy!
Yea! Even for this tears!

Little Lost Angel

A tiny baby angel,
Little and new and alone,
Going from Earth to Heaven,
Got lost in the great unknown.

Then God, in gracious pity,
Was troubled and sore distressed.
He sent out many searchers
And told them not to rest

Till the little baby angel
Was brought from the chilling cold.
The harps were hushed and waiting,
And quiet were the streets of gold.

But lightning was God's searchlight,
Thunder the hurrying horde
of angels seeking the lost one
To bring him home to the Lord.

And, after the search was ended,
Came rain, with its soothing sound.
Angels were shedding their happy tears
In joy that the lost was found.

A Woman Talks with God

I am alone, Dear God, one tiny atom in this
universe of yours.
I have my sorrows—more than ever I had thought
that I could bear—
But I have borne them, God, and found the shining
armor of my faith obscures
The pain. For as I meet the trials that you send, I
reap a judgment fair.

I have so much of gladness, Lord, I cannot count
my sorrows when I think
Of all the shining hours joy has brought. I have the
ones I love, and who love me.
They make my life a lengthening chain of joy, each
serving as a golden link
Which binds me close to Goodness and to Right.
Some are so near that I can see
Their gentle smiles, or reach out in tender love and
clasp their outstretched hands—
Others are so far away the miles are bruises on my
longing heart.
In spite, howe'er, of all the footsore, weary miles
that stretch between, Love spans
The distance as it were not there, and we are close,
though far apart.

Yet, what I think, and how I feel, my heart's
reaction to the daily world,

The dictates of my conscience, and the strength or weakness of my own free will,
Are mine—and mine alone—my inner self, my soul, is as a flag kept furled.

There are no words to tell. There are no windows of the soul. There is no skill
Which can be used to show myself to those most dear to me.
But You, Dear Lord,
To me You are the Love for others, in my heart, my King, upon a throne.
You are my very Life ... And yet, this is the cross I bear, this is my rod:
I am alone. With those I hold most dear, except for You, I am alone.

A Prayer

A mirror gives—it does not take.
There's nothing deep within.
It may be made of shining glass,
Or a polished piece of tin.

The calm, unruffled surface of
A mountain lake at noon
Reflects the sun until it's gone,
And then it holds the moon.

Lord, let me not a mirror be
That changes with each viewer.
I'd rather give a picture back
Of gray skies looking bluer.

Let me reflect Your perfect peace
To those who come my way,
Give comfort in their troubled times,
Share laughter when they're gay.

Let me hold deep within my heart
Each burden they might bring—
And guide them on to walk Your way,
With happy hearts that sing.

Brothers

You are a part of me
And I a part of you.
You are neither saint nor sinner,
And I am not Gentile nor Jew.

In His image were you made,
From clay the same as I.
His love fashioned both of us—
No one can break that tie.

One rose is white, another red.
One bird is drab, another bright.
We do not scorn one or the other,
But view them all with great delight.

So greet me only as your brother,
And I will love you as God's own.
Then there will be no shame to bear
When we meet at His great throne.

Scars

A brand-new doll I never chose,
I loved the one with chewed-up nose.
I still have scars from skinned-up knees
Battered and bruised from climbing trees.

Scars are signs of life to me.
I like to see a twisted tree
Lifting gnarled, yet patient arms
Defying hurt from future harms.

For sorrows borne throughout the years,
I waste no time in idle tears.
I thank the Lord for wounds that heal,
And know He lifts up those who kneel.

The Parade

Join the throng that marches onward
Through the jostling, pushing crowd.
Worldly people start to listen
To "hosannas" clear and loud.

And the ranks are growing daily
As the strong bring in the weak,
As the proud desert their world-ways .
For the ways of God's own meek.

There is peace upon their faces,
There is purpose in their tread.
They are not seeking fame or fortune—
Asking only daily bread.

Brave Sorrow

Her hands lay still and empty,
Her eyes were dull and red.
She asked about my mother
While her mother was just dead ...

My throat was tight and aching
As I gently bowed my head.
She asked about my mother
While her mother was just dead ...

Soldiers

My troubles come like soldiers—two by two,
Marching with grim faces to a weary war.
Nothing I say, nor anything I do
Can take from me these sorrows I abhor.

Yet, watching soldiers, with their faces grave,
Marching with steady stride to meet the foe,
I knew the joy that comes of being brave,
And felt the pride which those who fight may know.

The Dance

The faces all are different,
　　The eyes are not the same.
To some life's filled with sorrow,
　　To others it's a game.

One face is laughing through the dance,
　　And one is rapt and still.
One face is bright with happiness,
　　And one looks white and ill.

But all go swaying, dancing on
　　While death waits at the door,
To watch the bright and jewelled heels
　　Click on the glassy floor!

God Loves Variety

Examine all the things you see
And you will stand in awe.
No two-alikes are made by God—
No fish, or plant, or claw.

And so it is with you and me.
You are uniquely you,
And I am like no other.
We know that this is true.

I'm glad I'm I, and you are you.
So, I know you and you know me.
I'm glad He made us so.
I know God loves variety—and so do we!

Dead Dreams

I once had stopped for happy dreams
At a flower shop each day,
To choose the flowers for a bride
From the midst of the bright display.

But when I looked with haunted eyes
For the happy bride's bouquet,
I saw tube roses, waxen white,
Arranged in a funeral spray.

I Grieve

I grieve not for the ones I love
Who have gone on before.
I know they live in peace and joy
Beyond that secret door.

And I am sure that we shall meet
When I shall leave this life
So I rejoice that they are through
With all the pain and strife.

But there are things for which I grieve
And wish I could undo.
I do regret kind words unsaid,
And smiles which were too few.

I could have spent more leisure time
To give them happy hours.
We could have shared more songs of birds,
And picked more lovely flowers.

I know the Lord forgives my sins—
He cancels every one—
But I'll regret until I die
The things I have not done.

Comfort

The sordidness and bitter scalding tears
Fade with the passing of long-drawn years.
The gentle loving hands of God alone
Can ease the ache of sorrow that you've known.

Death of friend or loved one should be bravely borne
For though the heart with grief be sad and torn,
Your blessed Lord will heal the ragged wound,
And solace for your sorrow will be found.

His love will change to sweet the bitter rue,
And with the years He brings to you
The ecstasy of feeling changed to thought—
And you will know the peace which sorrow brought.

The Old and Sick

The sick and lonely need your love.
Their thoughts are much on dying.
Let them share in more of living,
And dry their eyes from crying.

Go! With a gladsome heart and smile.
Make them have a happy day.
Take part in their remembering,
And let your face be bright and gay.

Tell them your life is more complete
Because they've been within your heart.
And you will be the one most blest
When it is time to part.

I Have a Friend

I have a friend whom others criticize.
Perhaps they have a cause. I do not know.
She has the name of being cross, and mean,
And ugly in her face. Well, maybe so—

I only know when I was grieved and sad
And needed someone to be kind to me,
She was my friend. Now, when I look at her,
Her beauty is the only thing I see.

One Dream

My dream was growing rank and green,
With golden blossoms rare,
With many tender little buds
Waiting to open there.

Though it was Spring, the sun was warm,
And all things right for growing,
My dream felt touched on every side
By cold of winter blowing.

I put it in a sunny spot,
And tended it each day,
But still it died—as some dreams do—
So, I carried it away.

I put it in a lonely grave
And, with one little kiss,
I went to find another dream
To dry the tears for this.

Lost Joys

Yesterday, I hurried down life's busy way,
My mind intent upon my work at hand,
Nor stopped to notice, as I passed along
The beauties of the reawakening land.

Then, glancing by, I saw a little boy,
Quiet, small, and happy—by a murky pond.
His face was shining with his childhood joy,
His thoughts unruffled by the world beyond.

An unkept rose vine straggled by the way,
Its shaggy flowers by fierce thorns were banned.
But, by the vine, that grimy, barefooted boy,
A bunch of roses clutched in either hand!

And I, who am long grown from childhood days,
Knew man oft times is cheated of his goal
By harsh and constant will to not submit
To inborn softness in his wistful soul.

I yearn to find again the joy he has
In simple things. There is no way I can
Recapture them. I know it is too late.
But if he knew, the child would pity me, the man!

The Dark

I am afraid of the stealthy dark
   That fills the night with gloom.
It creeps into dim corners,
   And hides in an unused room.

All hunched and holding its sides
   It laughs with crazy glee;
And ever its groping, icy claws
   Grip at the heart of me!

I hear it bound with padded feet
   Across the polished floor—
While, tense with terror, my horror-filled eyes
   Stare at the waiting door!

Conversation

I find myself with ready quips
On each and all occasions.
I can make light of politics,
Or religious persuasions.

My scintillating wit comes forth
In charming platitudes.
I never leave a single doubt
About my attitudes.

And so, I wonder why it is,
Since I'm so very bright,
I only think, "I-should-have-said,"
When I'm alone at night!

Bored?

I'm never bored;
How could I be?
There's more to do,
And more to see,
And more to learn,
And more to be told
Than my short life
Can ever hold!

Children at School

The school room is a tiny world
With pupils of all kinds.
Some are the laggard and the slow
And some have crooked minds.
A few are likeable and good
And some repulse the heart.
But all will face their death at last,
With scars from living's mart.

One girl child has an elfin face
While in a thoughtful mood,
But her hands are witches' talon claws
And her speech is more than crude.
Another little girl is shy,
Her voice is soft and muffled.
Her frocks of baby pinks and blues,
Of pretty prints and ruffled.

Sitting next to her there is
A boy not quite sincere.
He'd like to play with girls and dolls,
But knows his mates would jeer.
There's one who whines and frowns a lot
She'll make a nagging wife—
And one I love, although his eyes
Shift when he faces strife.

One boy's a blue-eyed Viking
Who learns his lessons slow,
But runs and jumps and draws such cars
They look like they could go.
And one is dirty, one is vile,
And one is never still.
One comes to school all pale and thin,
With a pocket full of pills.

One rolls her eyes, and twists about
And never knows a thing.
Then there's a redhead with bright eyes
That flash like a bluebird's wing,
He has a million things for play,
From wheels out of the clock
To long green snakes in bottles
That give the girls a shock.

One has a face just like a horse,
And stutters when she reads.
And one will never learn a thing—
He should be chopping weeds.
One rides a skinny horse at home
And makes him buck and pitch,
And one will never learn to spell,
Another has the itch.

One girl is spoiled and wants her way,
Regardless of the cost.
I'm sure the man who marries her
Will find himself well bossed.
And one is roly-poly fat,
And one has floppy ears.

There's one whose father beats him so
That all the world he fears.

And so, Their different faces
I scan each day until
Sometimes I think of children all
I've surely had my fill.
But then I know that is not true,
For in this group I've found
Two children whom I call my own,
With eyes so big and round,

With faces clean and shining bright,
And mouths that laugh a lot.
I say it's true I want no child,
But know full well it's not.
I want a little blue eyed girl,
A boy to shyly smile,
To dress them up and send to school
To drive their teacher wild!

I Don't Like Cold

I woke one chilly winter morn
And rose to turn on heat,
Then crept back in my still-warn bed
To warm my icy feet.

I thought that on some future day
How cold would be my bed.
I felt a shiver up my spine
Just thinking of me dead.

The rains of Spring will not touch me,
Nor winter snows bring cold,
And I thanked God that then my soul
Would be in Heaven's fold,

And not encased in human form,
To feel with human senses.
I laughed to think that is one way
That old death recompenses!

Odds and Ends

Hence These Tears

I found a tube of glue upon my desk today.
The tube was new, the colors bright and gay.
Not thinking what I did, I scraped the paint away,
And underneath was lead, of shroud-like gray.
With death-fixed eyes, I saw my life in bare relief,
And felt my soul shrink back and bow its head in
grief.

Regret

I saw him vividly—I touched him physically.
We laughed—We cried—We shared the things we did.
He suffered terribly—I watched him yearningly,
Yet did not know the pain that he kept hid.

He died so gruesomely—I thought so suddenly.
I had not known Death claimed him for her own.
Though watching faithfully—Love failed so utterly,
And left him in his pain to die alone!

Shame

I found the sorrow of my friend so dear,
And looking back, I should have known her fear.
But no wind of ill had blown my way—
I had been gay and happy all the day.

I should have sensed her pain and grief,
And been close by the offer love's relief.
How could I not have known?
She bore her sadness all alone!

Laughter

Laughter can be a cruel thing
Unless it is soft as an angel's wing.
The savage laughs as he stalks through the night,
Seeking his prey in the dim moonlight.
And the hyena, laughing so tauntingly,
Through the deep jungle—stealthily—hauntingly,
Like the mocking laugh of ridicule
Flung in the face of the grinning fool!
The high thin cackle that turns us cold
As we sit by the bed of the very old—
And the fearful cry of the maniac
As he laughs, and laughs till his face is black.
There's the laugh of hate, and the laugh of fear,
And the laugh of the drunkard's foolish leer.
The murderer laughs at the bulging eye
Of the awful thing he has caused to die!
The hateful laugh comes at the end
Of an unkind joke on someone's friend.
And even the shout of the happy child
Is not so sweet as the Babe who smiles
At the mother's eyes, so tender with love
As she talked to Him of the God above,
Who is ever so patient, and tender, and kind
With those of the earth who are crippled and blind.

For we do not worship a laughing God,
But one who sadly wields His rod.
Laughter can be a cruel thing,

Unless it is soft as an angel's wing.
The hermit sits in his house alone,
And writes of the joys of the great white throne.
The priest does not tell of a laughing place,
But one ruled o'er by a sad, sweet face.
We cannot laugh of the things worthwhile,
But think of them with a tender smile,
And often times with a bitter tear
We greet some memory, sad, but dear.
The prophets old of ages past—
Commanded the people to pray and to fast,
And reverently worship, in silence and awe,
Ever fulfilling the holy law.
The mother cries in her wonderful joy
At the return of her prodigal boy.
We do not gaze with laughter gay
At the setting sun on a beautiful day.
We stand in sorrow, with bended head,
And pity the mother who sits with her dead—
And we think of Mary, the mother of God,
How even she must suffer the rod
Of One who is ever so patient and kind
With those of the earth who are crippled and blind.

For we do not worship a laughing God,
But one who sadly wields His rod.
Laughter can be a cruel thing,
Unless it is soft as an angel's wing.

Destiny

The osier willows nod and bow to the brook's waters as they hurry by. The waters give back small gurgling sounds, but pass them by with quiet disdain for willows nodding in the sun.

They have a date at some far distant shore with waiting seas. They cannot stop to pass the time of day in idle gossip about wind, and rain, and birds that come to drink, and stay to sing.

Their duty has been clearly marked; to go, with never ending diligence, to meet and blend with all the waters which they find, until at last stern destiny is done.

They merge with boundless seas and needs must beat against the unrelenting shores forever more—begging for another chance to stop and chat awhile with nodding willows which were left behind so long ago.

While there, the willows bow politely to new waters as they pass, never knowing that the ones who went before have now fulfilled their goal, and as reward, are wearing whitecaps on their heads.

Who wants to even dream of far off whitecaps when they are wearing bird nests in their hair?

The Tree House

I slept in a tree house
Next to a bird
And all night lon
He sang God's word.

He sang of contentment,
He sang of peace,
He sang of the wonders
That never shall cease.

I'll think of the tree house
When woes weigh me down,
And remember the songbird
Who promised a crown—

A crown to reward us
When this life is through
If we let the Lord guide us
In all things we do.